ARE YOU FINISHED AT 50?

by TONI GOFFE

First published in Great Britain by
Pendulum Gallery Press
56 Ackender Road, Alton, Hants GU34 1JS

© *TONI GOFFE 1989*

ARE YOU FINISHED AT 50?
ISBN 0-948912-05-7

REPRINTED 1988, 1989

PRINTED IN GREAT BRITAIN BY
UNWIN BROTHERS LTD, OLD WOKING, SURREY

"HAPPY BIRTHDAY TO YOU. HAPPY BIRTHDAY TO YOU......"

"FINISHED?! RUBBISH, I'M JUST HAVING A BREATHER!"

" WELL DEAR, YOU CAN STILL MANAGE IT — EVEN AT YOUR AGE....."-

" POOR OLD THING, I KNEW BLOWING OUT 50 CANDLES WOULD BE TOO MUCH FOR HIM ...... "-

"DON'T WORRY DEAR, IT ONLY COMES ROUND ONCE..."

"A LOT OF PEOPLE ARE FINISHED AT 50........
BUT NOT ME ...."-

" HE MAY BE 50, BUT HE STILL MANAGES TO GET TO THE PUB FOR A DRINK...."

" LOOK AT IT THIS WAY, YOU'RE LIKE TWO 25 YEAR
OLDS ROLLED INTO ONE ..... "-

"I THOUGHT IT WOULD BE BETTER THAN **50** CANDLES!"

" HELLO, HELLO, IT'S BIRTHDAY BOY HERE.....
GET YOUR PRESENTS READY..... "-

" I LIKE GEORGE, HE ALWAYS KNOWS WHEN HE'S HAD ENOUGH..."

" NOT BLOODY BURNT TOAST AGAIN?"

"MISS JONES, YOU'RE GOING TO HAVE TO GIVE ME FIVE MINUTES START....."

"HUM, I WONDER IF I COULD SWAP YOU FOR TWO 25 YEAR OLDS?"

"I HAVEN'T LEFT YOU, YOU IDIOT!
I'VE JUST BEEN **SHOPPING**!!"

" HE'S BEEN DEEPLY DISTURBED, SINCE HIS 50th BIRTHDAY! "

"MANY HAPPY RETURNS, MY LOVELY ONE....."

"BREAKFAST IN BED! WOW! THAT MEANS THAT I'VE FORGOTTEN SOMETHING I DID LAST NIGHT OR I SHOULD REMEMBER TO DO SOMETHING TONIGHT......"

-" WILL YOU STOP SMILING WHEN I'M CONCENTRATING "-

"NO, I HAVEN'T BEEN OUT YET, **THIS** IS JUST WITH TYING MY SHOE LACE.."

EXCERCISE IS WONDERFUL! EVERY MORNING I WALK BRISKLY.....
......TO THE CAR!

" JOB!? WHAT DO YOU WANT A JOB FOR AT YOUR AGE?".

"LET ME DO THAT, MISS JONES. THAT'S A MAN'S JOB!".

"JUST BECAUSE YOU LOOK LIKE AN ADVERT FOR A PENSION FUND DOESN'T MEAN YOU ARE ONE EH?"

"AH SEX, YES, I REMEMBER THAT!"

" AWAKE SLEEPING BEAUTY, YOUR PRINCE CHARMING
HAS ARRIVED ....

" HERE'S YOUR BREAKFAST, TIGER!....."

" WHAT'S THAT IN REAL·OLD· MONEY ?.... ".

— " I STILL JOG .... DOWN TO THE PUB! ".

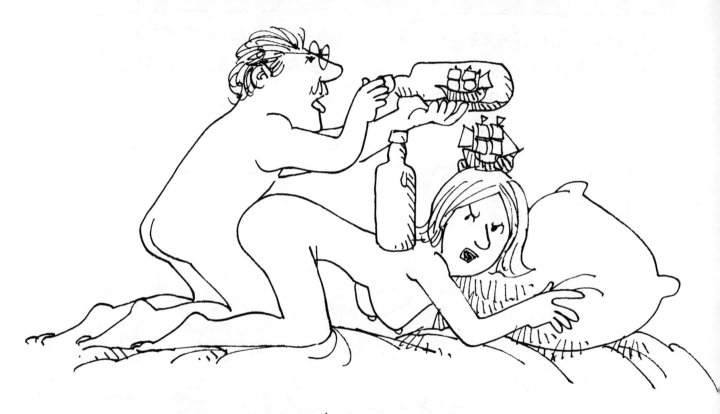

-" TUESDAY NIGHT! IS HOBBIES NIGHT,
DAVID, NOT SATURDAYS!"

"I CAN'T REMEMBER THE NAME OF WHOEVER IT WAS PHONED ASKING YOU ABOUT SOMETHING OR OTHER .... IMPORTANT.'"

MY WIFE'S JUST LEFT ME....
OHNO! FRED, HOW AWFUL, HAVE A DRINK
THANKS, YEAH SHE'S PICKING ME UP AFTER SHE'S BEEN SHOPPING....

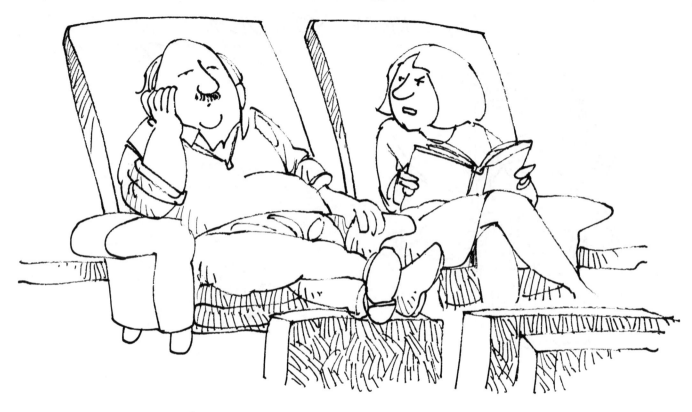

-" WAKE UP! IT'S TIME TO GO TO BED...."-

"DID YOU REMEMBER TO TAKE THE DOG OUT FOR HIS WALK TODAY?".

" IT'S THESE ROMANTIC MOMENTS OF THE AFTERMATH I SAVOUR ANGELA?".

"TAKE NO NOTICE, HE'S JUST GOING THROUGH HIS SECOND, SECOND CHILDHOOD.....!"-

-"I'M SORRY DEAR, I JUST CAN'T FIND IT, HAND ME
THE TORCH!"-

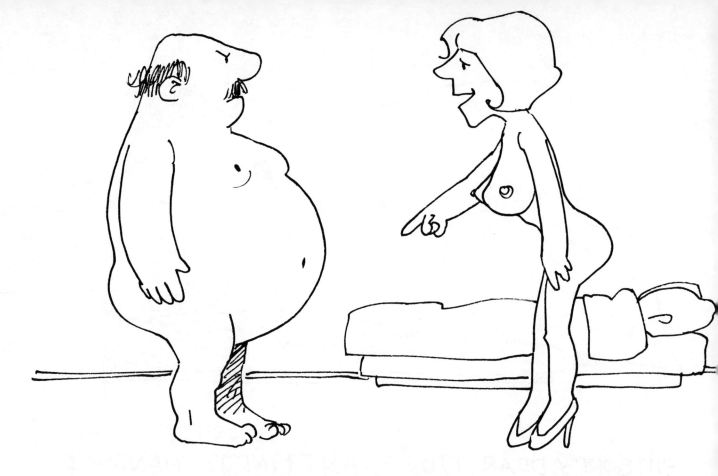

" I TOLD YOU IT WOULD   NEVER GROW IN THE SHADE!"

– "WELL, Mr JOHNSON, YOU'RE FULL OF LITTLE SURPRISES ARN'T YOU?" –

—"HAVEN'T SEEN YOU SINCE WE WERE AT SCHOOL
TOGETHER, YOU HAVEN'T CHANGED A BIT!"

"IT MUST BE WONDERFUL TO HAVE ALL THE KNOWLEDGE
YOU MUST HAVE GAINED, IN ALL THE TIME YOU'VE BEEN
AROUND......"

" IF HE WAS RIGID , I WOULD'NT BE FRIGID ".

" I SAID,' I THOUGHT THERE WAS MUSIC HERE!'"

"YOU KNOW WHAT I MISS ZELDA, TRYING TO DO THIS QUIETLY, SO NOT TO WAKE THE CHILDREN...."

-" GRANDAD, WHEN I'M BIG LIKE YOU, CAN I BUY
MAGAZINES WITH GIRLS LIKE THIS IN ? ".

"GRANDMA, TELL ME ABOUT WHEN YOU WERE A HIPPY....."

" GRANDAD, TELL ME ABOUT YOU AND THE
SWINGING 60's......."

"HAVE YOU EVER BEEN UNFAITHFUL TO ME HILDA?"

-"ASK MY WIFE TO PASS THE SALT, PLEASE!"-

-" OH NO! MY BACK'S GONE "-

" YOU KNOW WHAT ARTHUR, YOU'RE NO FUN ON THE BEACH ANYMORE......."

-"WE WOULD HAVE DIVORCED YEARS AGO, BUT WE NEVER SEEMED TO GET ROUND TO IT...."-

" THAT WAS A MIND BLOWING DOCUMENTARY,
N'EST PAS ? ".

-"TOP OF THE POPS IS ON DEAR!"-

I'VE LOST MY GLASSES. CAN I BORROW YOUR GLASSES SO I CAN LOOK FOR MY GLASSES....
THESE ARE YOUR GLASSES, I'VE LOST MY GLASSES WHEN I FOUND YOUR GLASSES...

"HOLD IT STEADY, JILL IT'S HARD ENOUGH DOING JUST ONE THING AT A TIME......."

—"LETTUCE ON A BED OF LETTUCE — AGAIN?"

GEORGE, YOU'RE STILL A ROMANTIC
OLD THING, YOU KNOW

"IF YOU HAVE HALF AS MUCH FUN AS I'VE HAD WHEN YOU'RE MY AGE, I'LL HAVE HAD TWICE AS MUCH FUN AS YOU....."

"IF YOU PUT YOUR COLD FEET ON MINE ONCE MORE, SOMEONE HERE IS GOING TO FIND IT HARD TO MAKE 51!!"-

"AH, IT'S GOOD TO GET AWAY FROM ALL THAT SEX AND DRUGS AND ROCK AND ROLL FOR A WHILE IS'NT DEAR?"

"I'VE ALWAYS BEEN A ONE WOMAN MAN MATILDA,
BUT I'M NOT SURE YOU'RE THE ONE...."

" HURRY UP BACK! "

"SORRY, MA'AM THIS IS ALL WE HAVE IN EVENING DRESSES......".

"GEORGE, I'VE BEEN YOUR WIFE FOR 28 YEARS AND I'VE ALWAYS BEEN A **VEGETARIAN**!"

"COMING TO BED EARLY TONIGHT WAS A GREAT IDEA — SARAH!!"—

"GEORGE. DO WE KNOW WHERE THIS YOUNG MAN AND HIS GIRL FRIEND CAN SCORE SOME COKE?".

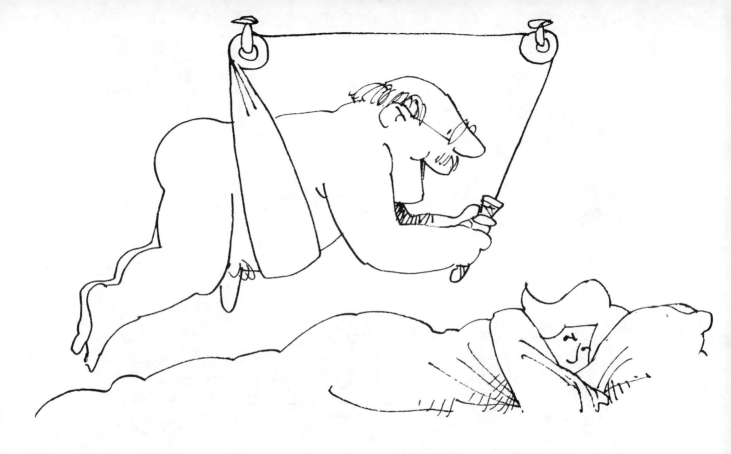

-" WITH ONE MIGHTY LEAP, YOUR LOVER IS AT YOUR SIDE...."-

"I WISH I HAD THE COURAGE TO SWITCH OFF SOMETIMES!"

ONE DAY, I'M GOING OUT AND BUY ALL THE VIDEOS OF ALL THE FILMS. I'VE SLEPT THROUGH THE ENDS OF, AND WATCH THEM ALL.......
THAT'S IF YOU DON'T FALL ASLEEP....
THE END

"OH WE'RE INTO GARDENING, WINEMAKING AND GROUP SEX ...."

"I DON'T KNOW WHY YOU'RE UNHAPPY, PERHAPS YOU SHOULD GO HOME TO YOUR HUSBAND...."

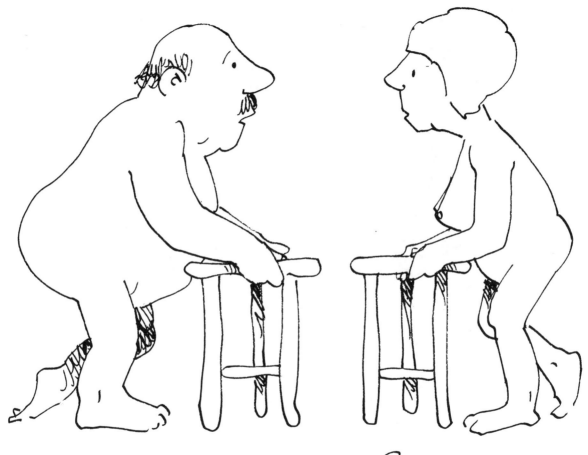

" NOW WHAT? "

"HELLO! IS THERE ANYTHING ALIVE DOWN THERE?"